**Please check all items for damages
before leaving the Library.
Thereafter you will be held
responsible for all injuries
to items beyond reasonable wear.**

Do You Share?

by Joanne Mattern

Reading consultant: Susan Nations, M.Ed., author/
literacy coach/consultant in literacy development

WEEKLY READER®
PUBLISHING

Please visit our web site at: www.garethstevens.com
For a free color catalog describing our list of high-quality books,
call 1-800-542-2595 (USA) or 1-800-387-3178 (Canada).

Library of Congress Cataloging-in-Publication Data

Mattern, Joanne.
  Do you share? / Joanne Mattern.
    p. cm. — (Are you a good friend?)
  Includes bibliographical references and index.
  ISBN-10: 0-8368-8275-X (lib. bdg.)
  ISBN-13: 978-0-8368-8275-9 (lib. bdg.)
  ISBN-10: 0-8368-8280-6 (softcover)
  ISBN-13: 978-0-8368-8280-3 (softcover)
  1. Sharing in children—Juvenile literature. 2. Friendship
in children—Juvenile literature. I. Title.
  BF723.S428M378   2008
  177'.62—dc22
                                                    2007011023

First published in 2008 by
Weekly Reader® Books
An imprint of Gareth Stevens Publishing
1 Reader's Digest Road
Pleasantville, NY 10570-7000 USA

Copyright © 2008 by Gareth Stevens, Inc.

Editor: Gini Holland
Art direction: Tammy West
Graphic designer: Dave Kowalski
Picture research: Diane Laska-Swanke
Photographer: Gregg Andersen
Production: Jessica Yanke

Printed in the United States of America

1 2 3 4 5 6 7 8 9 11 10 09 08 07

Note to Educators and Parents

Reading is such an exciting adventure for young children! They are beginning to integrate their oral language skills with written language. To encourage children along the path to early literacy, books must be colorful, engaging, and interesting; they should invite the young reader to explore both the print and the pictures.

The *Are You a Good Friend?* series is designed to help children learn the special social skills they need to make and keep friends in their homes, schools, and communities. The books in this series teach the social skills of listening, sharing, helping others, and taking turns, showing readers how and why these skills help establish and maintain good friendships.

Each book is specially designed to support the young reader in the reading process. The familiar topics are appealing to young children and invite them to read — and reread — again and again. The full-color photographs and enhanced text further support the student during the reading process.

In addition to serving as wonderful picture books in schools, libraries, homes, and other places where children learn to love reading, these books are specifically intended to be read within an instructional guided reading group. This small group setting allows beginning readers to work with a fluent adult model as they make meaning from the text. After children develop fluency with the text and content, the books can be read independently. Children and adults alike will find these books supportive, engaging, and fun!

— Susan Nations, M.Ed., author, literacy coach,
and consultant in literacy development

Are you a good friend? One way to be a good friend is to **share**. Do you know how to share?

5

There are many ways to share. Sometimes, sharing means making sure everyone gets a **piece**.

Sometimes, sharing means doing things together.
You can share toys.

You can share a **snack** with a friend. Sharing can be yummy!

11

You can share crayons.
There are plenty of colors
for two.

You can share dress-up clothes. Playing dress-up is so much fun when you share.

15

Sometimes, sharing is hard. Sometimes, you do not feel like sharing.

You and your friend can both feel good when you find a way to share.

Sharing is one way to **solve** problems. Sharing shows you care. Sharing is a great way to be a good friend!

Glossary

piece — part of something

share — to use something together

snack — a small meal or treat

solve — to find an answer to
a problem

For More Information

Sometimes I Share. Carol Nicklaus (Sterling)

Why Not Share? Janine Amos
    (Cherrytree Books)

Why Should I Share? Claire Llewellyn
    (Barron's Educational)

Your Fair Share. You and Me (series).
    Denise M. Jordan (Heinemann Library)

Index

About the Author

Joanne Mattern has written more than 150 books for children. Joanne also works in her local library. She lives in New York State with her husband, three daughters, and assorted pets. She enjoys animals, music, reading, going to baseball games, and visiting schools to talk about her books.